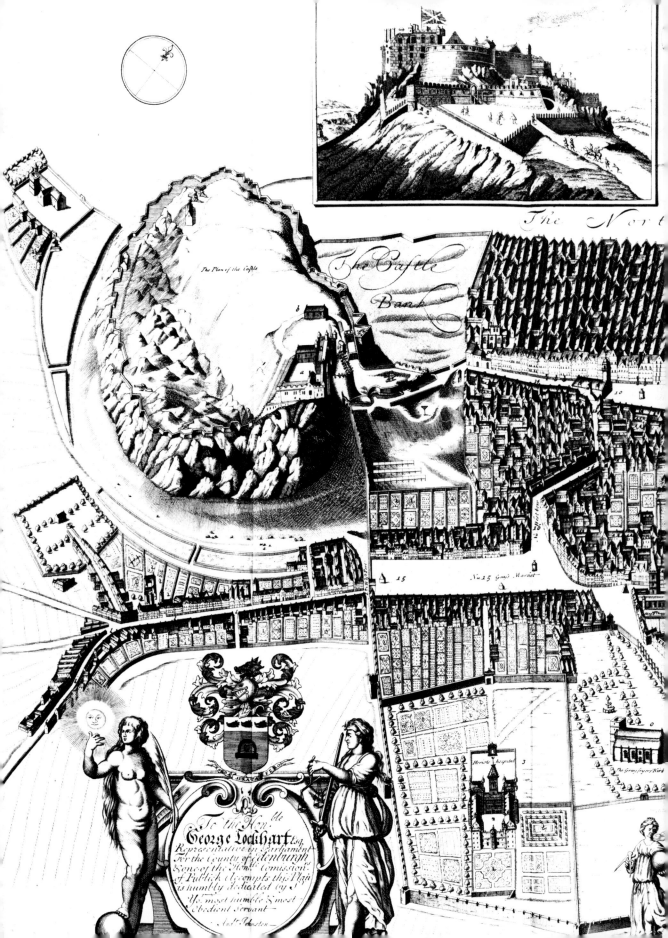

The Nort

The Plan of the Castle

The Castell Bank

Nᵒ 15 Graß Market

Herreots Hospitall 3

The Grayfryrs Kirk

To the Honᵇˡᵉ
George Lockhart Esqʳ
Representative in Parliament
For the County of Edenburgh
& one of the Honᵇˡᵉ Comißioners
of Publick Accompts this Plan
is humbly dedicated by
Yᵉ most humble & most
Obedient Servant
Andᵗ Johnston

The Buildings of Edinburgh

Anthony F. Kersting
and
Maurice Lindsay

B. T. BATSFORD LTD
LONDON

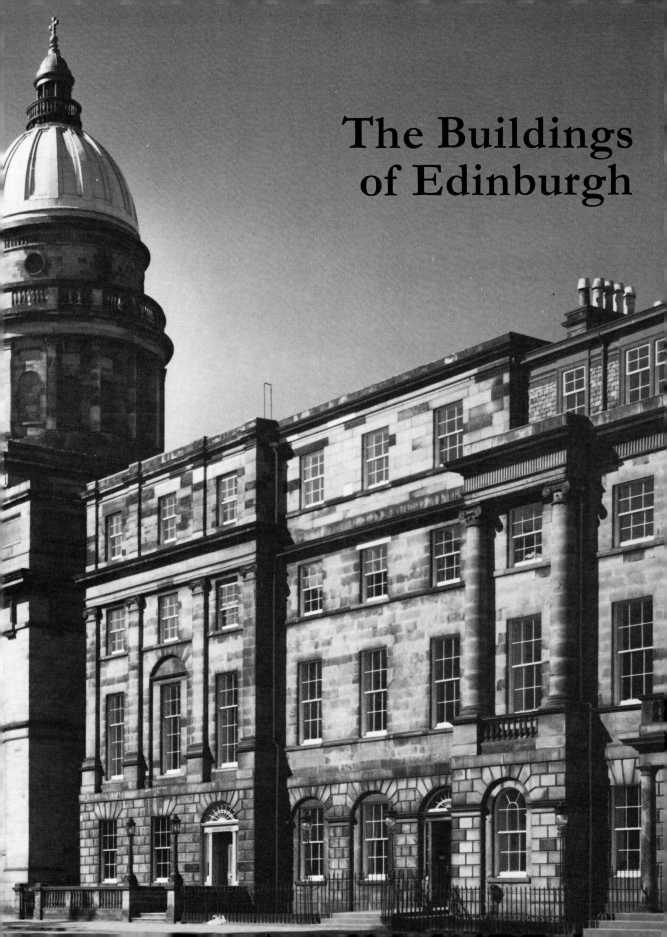

The Buildings
of Edinburgh

ISBN 0 7134 0875 8

Typeset in Monophoto Garamond,
11 on 13pt
and printed in Great Britain by
BAS Printers Limited, Over Wallop, Hants
for the publishers B. T. Batsford Ltd.
4 Fitzhardinge Street, London WIH OAH

The illustrations on the endpapers are: *front*
'The Plan of Edenburgh exactly done. From
the original of the famous D. Wit' *c.* 1724;
back James Craig's Plan of the New Town,
1767 (by courtesy of Edinburgh City
Libraries)

Title page illustration   St George's Church,
designed by Robert Reid in 1814 to
complete the vista at the west end of
George Street. Its dome was modelled on
that of St Paul's Cathedral. Gutted and
converted, it is now an extension to
Register House

Contents

Edinburgh: An Introduction

From the earliest times Edinburgh has attracted settlers as a place of dependable safety. The shelving ice-masses and floods of the various glacial epochs carved and washed out the raised site that later became the structural centrepiece of Scotland's Capital. The Royal Mile, stretching from the Castle at the top end to Holyroodhouse at the bottom, is made up of clay and gravel piled high by the irresistible force of ice-packs grinding round the base of the Castle rock. Britons, Romans and Picts made of Edinburgh a place of government and its Gaelic name, *Dun Eadain* (Fort of the Hill Slope), indicates the Celts' appreciation of its inherent defensive qualities. Whether the modern name derives from this source, or from the fact that early in the seventh century the Saxon king who overthrew the Picts of Dunedin was Edwin of Northumbria, is of little moment. Although rivalled at various times by Perth (or Sanct Johnstoun, to give it its old name), Dunfermline and Stirling, Edinburgh assumed the role of capital city in a Scotland more or less united for the first time in the eleventh century.

It is predominantly a hilly city. Arthur's Seat, Edinburgh's Formorian 'giant of three heads', was so named in the fifteenth century when the Arthurian romances became popular at the Scottish court; Salisbury Crags, titled with unaccountable generosity after that Earl of Salisbury who was a commander in the invading army of Edward III; and Calton Hill, the site of those 'chill pillars of fluted stone' (as Douglas Young called them) that are the principal monuments to Edinburgh's 'Athens of The North' phase; Blackford Hill, with its stone quarries and its observatory; Corstorphine Hill and, most central and prominent of them all, the Castle rock.

As a result of this plethora of eminences, Edinburgh is a city of spectacular vistas, though the most easily enjoyed and the widest ranging are those to be seen from the ramparts of the Castle.

Appropriately, the oldest building in the city is perched on the summit of the Castle rock, its position exaggerated by the cutting away of surrounding rock for the making of a road in the sixteenth century. St Margaret's Chapel was built about 1090 by Queen Margaret, wife of Malcolm Canmore. The masonry is Norman; dressed rectangular blocks of freestone above and below which is later work of rubble. Inside, somewhat surprisingly, is a semi-circular stone-vaulted apse. The vault of the nave dates from the 1840s, though the arch between nave and apse was constructed in the time of Margaret's son, David I. The chapel as a whole is a declaration in miniature of the confident faith.

Sir Robert Lorimer's adjacent National War Memorial, built in the 1920s, has thus to stand somewhat unfair comparison. Though magnificently crafted, it is not a chapel. Perhaps partly for this reason it creates a feeling of uneasiness; the self-conscious tribute of an already sceptical age to those who fell in what was supposed to be 'the war to end wars'.

Across the Palace yard – or Close, to give it its old name – is James IV's Great Hall, now a display centre for a spectacular array of armour set against a Gothic screen. The vault or Casemates beneath were used as a prison during the Napoleonic wars.

The east side of the Close carries the Royal Palace. In its present form it owes much to James VI and I, who was born in it. He had it remodelled and improved for his visit to Scotland in 1617, 14 years after he had mounted the English throne. The King's Lodging had its panelling and moulded plaster ceilings stripped by Cromwell, who besieged the Castle in 1650. He did not, however, mutilate the little room where the king was born, the royal monograms and the date when Mary, Queen of Scots bore him – 19 June 1566 – surviving on the painted wooden panels of walls and ceiling.

The Half-Moon Bastion, which faces down the High Street, was built by the Regent Morton on the foundation of a fourteenth-century tower put up by David II. It is from this Bastion that the one o'clock gun is fired every week-day. The idea was a Parisian one, and when instituted in 1869, no doubt dangerously startled visitors in a quieter age than our own, though its purpose was to enable the good burghers of the City in pre-radio times to check the accuracy of their watches.

The Old Town of Edinburgh reaches down the ribbed spine of the Royal Mile from the Castle to the Palace of Holyroodhouse, which replaced the Castle as the Scottish home of the later Stewarts and is still the sovereign's home in Scotland's Capital. The Old Town was described by Carlyle as covering 'like some wrought tissue of stone and mortar, like some rhinoceros skin, with many a gnarled embossment, church steeple, chimney head, Tolbooth and other ornament and indispensability, back and ribs of the slope.' On the whole the image of the Old Town as a rhinoceros skin is not one that has endeared itself to Edinburgh folk.

The earliest houses up and down the High Street were constructed of wood and wattle. Scotland did not take generally to the use of stone for domestic building until the sixteenth century. Indeed, Froissart tells us that when the French troops of Sir John de Vienne were in Scotland supporting Robert III in 1383, a house that had been burned by the English enemy could be rebuilt in two or three days with 'six posts and some branches'.

A century later houses with wooden frames of plaster or clay infilling, their gables often edging to the street, and set in long sloping hillside gardens, lined the High Street. None has survived.

By the beginning of the next century, the first of the lands or tenements, copied from mediaeval Europe, were being erected inside the sloping walled City. As the wynds and closes were squeezed more tightly together, the garden spaces were used up until there was no option but to build still further upwards. A fire of 1532 destroyed many of the highest of the early lands, but in 1636 the English traveller Sir William Brereton recorded that a number of new houses were still being 'faced with boards'.

One of the oldest houses to survive, the core of which was probably built about 1550, is Gladstone's Land, in the Lawnmarket (where the wool was once sold). It was acquired and extended in 1620 by a wealthy merchant, Thomas Gladstone, an ancestor of the future British prime minister, W. E. Gladstone. The house was restored in the 1930s by Sir Frank Mears for the National Trust for Scotland, and is now furnished in the manner of its period as a social museum, open to the public. Like many houses of its time it has painted ceilings, probably the work of Italian craftsmen.

Between the Castle and the Lawnmarket some other old houses survive, though with altered interiors. There is, for instance, Cannonball House, built by a furrier called Mure in 1630, with a Jacobite cannonball embedded in the wall facing the Castle and – a common Scots practice – a religious motto, 'O Lord in Thee is al mi Traist', engraved over the lintel. Others include the Outlook Tower building, strong in its associations with that pioneer of town planning Sir Patrick Geddes; and opposite, Boswell's Court, where in 1773 Dr Samuel Johnson was taken by James Boswell to visit one of Bozzy's medical relations.

Lower down, where the Assembly Hall of the Church of Scotland and its related complex now backs, was once the splendid Palace of Mary of Lorraine, its destruction in 1846 heralding a wave of so-called 'improving' modernisation that was to sweep away much of value and character during the ensuing century.

Across the street, Tolbooth St John's, known as the Highland Church, is a good example of early Victorian Pointed, built in 1842 by James Gillespie Graham.

When the Old Town gardens had to be sacrificed to make way for further building, the construction of courts entered by pends off the High Street began. Mylne's Court, put up by a member of the family who for generations were master masons to the Scottish kings in the days before there was an architectural profession, went up in 1690. It is part demolished, part restored as a University residence. James's Court, the work of a speculative builder, contained in its western block (now burned down), the home of the philosopher David Hume. Wardrop's Court includes a particularly handsome land, well restored and internally modernised at the behest of one of the Dukes of Hamilton. The heavily Victorianised Lady Stair's House, now a literary museum housing relics of Burns, Scott and Stevenson, crouches between Mylne's Court and Wardrop's Court. Riddle's Court, across the High Street, holds what was the philosopher David Hume's first Edinburgh home. Brodie's Close commemorates the notorious Deacon Brodie, respectable citizen by day but burglar by night and the prototype of Stevenson's story 'Dr Jekyll and Mr Hyde'.

The Capital's North Bridge, constructed in 1767 and the first breach in the close-packed old Town, together with the South Bridge, which was constructed to the Canongate between 1826 and 1836, mark off the central section of the Old Town. This contains St Giles's Cathedral, with its spectacular crown steeple completed in 1495 and repaired by John Mylne in 1648. The Reformers treated St Giles roughly. Mass was sung for the last time in 1560. John Knox – that spiritual founding father and literary embodiment of Scottish intolerance – had preached his first sermon there the previous year, after which its altars were torn out, its fine glass destroyed and its ritual furnishings sold.

The four octagonal pillars in the transept supporting the tower are probably part of the previous twelfth-century chapel on the site, as are those in the choir. Of its chapels, the Albany Aisle has been adapted as a memorial to the men and women of the congregation who fell in two World Wars. The Hammermen's Chapel, near the north choir, carries the last guild banner of Edinburgh's Hammermen. The Preston Aisle, at the south east corner of the church, dates from 1453 (though it was enlarged 12 years later) and has a beautiful groined roof. It once housed the arm bone of St Giles – a relic that disappeared during the Reformation – and was the scene of the signing of the Solemn League and Covenant of 1643. The Chepman Aisle, to the south west, was granted to the printer Walter Chepman (Scotland's Caxton), for him to erect an altar. It now contains a monument to the great Marquis of Montrose who, with his captain, Hay of Dalgetty, lies buried in the vaults below. The Moray Aisle has a monument to Mary, Queen of Scots's half-brother James, Earl of Moray, and a window by the Pre-Raphaelite artist Sir Noel Paton commemorating the Regent Moray's assassination at Linlithgow. Finally, inaugurated in 1911 and designed by Sir Robert Lorimer (to whom there is a memorial in the Preston Aisle) there is the Chapel of the Most Ancient and Most Noble Order of the Thistle, containing what is probably the most elaborately and beautifully carved Gothic work to be carried out in Scotland since the Middle Ages.

St Giles has suffered many internal viscissitudes over the centuries as well as a necessary but badly executed external restoration by William Burn in 1829. Divided into four churches after the Reformation, together with a meeting-place for the judges of the Supreme Court, it became an Episcopal Cathedral in 1633 and remained so until 1638. The stool-throwing episode of the probably fictitious Jenny Geddes ('Dost thou say Mass in my lug?') of 1637 once again heralded evil times for the building. By 1643 a vault was being used as a powder magazine, and later, parts of the building became a prison and a police office.

The Capital's Parliament Close (or Square) has a fine statue of the merry monarch Charles II on horseback, placed in position in 1685 almost exactly over the bones of the gloomy Reformer, John Knox; a happy circumstance more likely in Scotland to have been accidental than a manifestation either of humour or poetic justice.

Parliament House was completed in 1639. The Scottish Parliament had hitherto met in the Old Tolbooth – featured in Scott's *The Heart of Midlothian* – pulled down in 1829. The new building has an imposing Great Hall, magnificently timbered with arched and trussed oak beams. Less than a century later it was to echo to the debates that led to the Act of Union of 1707 and 'the end of ane auld sang', as Lord Seafield, one of those whose votes had been bought with English bribe-money, contemptuously called the legal instrument. The Capital's Supreme Law Court of Scotland took over Parliament House when the politicians left it. Today, it stands behind the pleasant classical façade added by Sir Robert Reid in 1808.

Facing the restored Mercat Cross, re-erected at the expense of William Ewart Gladstone in 1885, is the City Chambers, built between 1753 and 1761 as the Royal Exchange.

Christ's Church at the Tron, begun in 1637 and named after the old public weighing beam, had a bell celebrated in verse by Edinburgh's eighteenth-century laureate, Robert Fergusson. The bell was lost in the fire that consumed the steeple in 1824, a blaze watched by Sir Walter Scott and Lord Cockburn. The spire was replaced and the Church continued in use until 1952. Threatened with demolition by a developer, it was purchased by the Secretary of State for Scotland and given to the City. Restored externally, it still awaits a new use.

At the foot of Niddry Street is the well-restored St Cecilia's Hall of 1762. It housed Edinburgh's earliest public concerts, including probably the first public performance in Scotland of Handel's 'Messiah'.

Off the High Street again, Anchor Close was the location of the printing presses of William Smellie, who edited the first edition of the *Encyclopaedia Brittanica*, published between 1768 and 1771. It was also a home of George Drummond who, when Lord Provost, led the City into the adventure of building the New Town. He has been referred to, somewhat unfairly, as the 'Haussmann of Edinburgh', though his motives had certainly no sinister military significance.

In Carrubber's Close, where Old St Paul's is situated, Allan Ramsay, the poet whose statue stands at the foot of The Mound, opened his theatre in 1736. Moubray House is said to be the oldest in the City, dating from about 1451. The so-called John Knox's house dates from the sixteenth century and is the last timber-galleried house in Edinburgh; but its tradition as the scene of the death of the famous Reformer is probably apocryphal; a legendary confusion of Knoxes, perhaps.

Tweeddale Court is a mansion built by Dame Margaret Kerr, the founder of Lady Yester's Church. Now owned by the local authority, it is presently in a shameful state of unused neglect.

The lowest stretch of the Royal Mile is known as the Canongate or 'way of the Cannons Regular' of the Order of St Augustine. To have sought refuge within the precincts of this religious order at one time ensured protection against arrest for debt, the Canongate's stature as a separate burgh surviving until 1856.

The Canongate managed to retain more of its old houses than the rest of the High Street. One of the best of them, Morocco's Land, all but collapsed in the heavy snowfall of 1948; but there have been notable restorations and sensitive replacements. White Horse Close, once a coaching inn, and 11 to 15 Canongate are among the most noteworthy. Shoemakers' Land, built in 1677, and the the surrounding blocks, have also been well restored. The gap left by Morocco's Land has been infilled by the architect Robert Hurd echoing the old buildings and copying the Scottish frontal arcades or piazzas that now survive in the original only in Gladstone's Land.

Acheson House, built for a Secretary of State to Charles I, dates from 1633, and has become the headquarters of an organisation marketing the products of Scottish craftsmen. Over the pend of Bakehouse Close stands Huntly House, bearing the date 1570 and now a city museum. Moray House, its gateway flanked by twin pyramids, was built by Mary, Countess of Home in 1628, but passed to her daughter, the Countess of Moray. It is now a small part of a large teachers' training college.

The most substantial of these Canongate mansions is Queensberry House. Sold to the government by the eccentric 'Old Q' (Wordsworth's 'Degenerate Douglas! Oh the unworthy lord!') for a barracks, it is now a home for ex-servicemen.

Two of the Canongate's other public buildings also survive in remarkable condition; the Tolbooth, dated 1592 but which has an outsize Victorian clock slung round its neck; and Canongate Church, built in 1688 by James VII and II to house the displaced congregation when he turned the Abbey Church of Holyrood, then partly in use as a Parish Church, into a Chapel Royal. The Canongate pulpit was once occupied by Dr Thomas Chalmers, who led the 1843 Disruption in the Church of Scotland. Amongst those who rest in its graveyard is the young Edinburgh poet Robert Fergusson, over whose grave stands a headstone commissioned and paid for – it cost five pounds and ten shillings (50p) – by Fergusson's great successor in the eighteenth-century literary revival, Robert Burns.

At the foot of the Royal Mile is Holyroodhouse. The Holyrood of the Jameses was a simpler building than the fine structure Sir William Bruce built for Charles II. The present mansion never really fulfilled its royal purpose, though it did shelter the exiled Charles X of France for some years and still houses members of the British Royal Family when they visit Edinburgh.

The Abbey was founded by Queen Margaret's son David I around 1178, the outline of the original structure being marked by stones in the grass. Only the roofless nave of the church and a square tower remain standing. The Earl of Hertford wreaked damage on it (as well as on the great Border Abbeys) in 1544. One of James V's bastard sons was given the Abbacy, and proceeded to build himself a house with the stones. The fanatical followers of the Protestant Earl of Glencairn did some further wrecking in 1567. Eventually, it was sufficiently repaired for James VI to be married in. James VII's attempt to convert it to a Chapel Royal, with stalls for his revived Knights of the Thistle, meant that in due course it automatically atttracted the destructive energies of the followers of his son-in-law, William of Orange, not even the royal coffins being spared. An eighteenth-century attempt to re-roof the fabric resulted in its final collapse, to the frail shell we have inherited today.

Cromwell's troops saw to it that there was an accidental fire at Holyrood; hence Charles II's employment of Sir William Bruce, the first great Scottish architect known to us as such by name. James IV's tower was partnered by Bruce's new one, and Sir William's Renaissance classicism was not too unkind to the earlier remains.

The coffered ceiling of Queen Mary's apartment remains much as it was in her day. So, too, do Darnley's apartments on the floor beneath. The long gallery retains its images of 110 Scottish kings, real and imaginary from Fergus II to Charles II, commissioned from a Dutch painter, de Weet, at two pounds per king.

Life in the basically mediaeval Old Town was cosy, overcrowded but relatively classless, lords, professional men and tradesmen living in different flats of the same land. After 1746 the City's defensive needs seemed to belong to the past. The idea of a New Town on the other side of Nor' Loch, a much-drained odoriferous marsh where Waverley Station stands, was envisaged by Daniel Defoe in the 1720s, when he published the third volume of his *Tour Thro' the whole Island of Great Britain*. There, he remarked:

> The City suffers infinite Disadvantages, and lies under such scandalous Inconveniences as are, by its Enemies, made a Subject of Scorn and Reproach; as if the People were not as willing to live sweet and clean as other Nations, but delighted in Stench and Nastiness: whereas, were any other People to live under the same Unhappiness, I mean as well of a rocky and mountainous Situation, throng'd Buildings, from seven to ten or twelve storey high, a Scarcity of Water, and that little they have difficult to be had, and to the uppermost Lodgings, far to fetch; we should find a *London*, or a *Bristol* as dirty as *Edinburgh*, and, perhaps, less able to make their Dwelling tolerable, at least in so narrow a Compass; for tho' many Cities have more People in them, yet, I believe, this may be said with Truth, that in no City in the World so many People live in so little Room as at *Edinburgh*.
>
> On the North Side of the City is a spacious, rich, and pleasant Plain, extending from the Lough, which joins the City, to the River of *Leith*, at the mouth of which

is the Town of *Leith*, at the distance of a long *Scots* mile from the City. And even here, were not the North side of the Hill, which the City stands on, so exceedingly steep, as hardly, (at least to the Westward of their Flesh-market) to be clamber'd up on Foot much less to be made passable for Carriages. But, I say, were it not so steep, and were the Lough fill'd up as it might easily be, the City might have been extended upon the Plain below, and fine beautiful Streets would, no Doubt, have been built there; nay, I question much, whether, in Time, the high Streets would not have been forsaken, and the City, as we might say, run all out of its Gates to the North. . .

A competition to decide layout plans was organised in 1766. George Drummond, six times Lord Provost of Edinburgh, was the prime mover. A young architect, James Craig, produced the winning scheme, and although his plan was subsequently modified, work started the following year.

The building of the Capital's New Town of Edinburgh, some might say the largest, most coherent and finest piece of planned townscape of the period in Europe, continued until 1833, soon after George IV's death, when the City became insolvent. The Georgian impetus, however, carried the work on into the Victorian period. In all there were seven phases in the construction of Edinburgh's New Town. Eventually, it was to cover more than 700 acres of finely ordered and distinctive architecture, punctuated by towers and spires and varied by gardens and green spaces.

The first phase of the New Town was bounded on the north by Queen Street and on the south by Princes Street. St Andrew Square marked the east end of the central axis of George Street, and Charlotte Square the west end. In between these main streets, Rose Street and Thistle Street were designed to accommodate coach houses, tradesmen's homes, shops and small businesses. The hard golden-grey stone came from Craigleith Quarry, west of the new city, and the slates from the West Highlands, mostly from Ballachulish. Notable individual buildings include the Royal Bank in St Andrew Square, built as the home of a Lord Provost, Sir Laurence Dundas, by Sir William Chambers; Register House by Robert Adam; St Andrew's Church in George Street, its circular design by a Major Fraser of the Royal Engineers, and St George's Church in Charlotte Square, now converted as an extension to Register House. Most of the domestic architecture was fairly plain – 'low Georgian' one might say – although 8 Queen Street by Robert Adam, 26 St Andrew Square and North Castle Street, in No. 39 of which Sir Walter Scott had his town house from 1802 to 1826, are distinguished. Finest of all is the Assembly Rooms building, on the south side of George Street, paid for by public subscription between 1784 and 1787 to plans by John Henderson. The Tuscan portico in front and the Music Hall behind were added by William Burn in 1843. It was in the splendid original hall of the building that at a dinner of the Edinburgh Theatrical Fund on 23 February 1827 Sir Walter Scott, who was a guest, allowed Lord Meadowbank declare the identity of the 'Great Unknown' as the author of the Waverley Novels. Scott, then still suffering from the sadness of his financial collapse (due to the indiscretion of his partners and his own lack of business acumen) was given tumultuous acclamation. From 1947 to 1980 the Assembly Rooms became well known to many visitors to Edinburgh as the home of the Edinburgh Festival Club during the City's annual International Festival of Music and Drama.

The finest domestic ranges are to be found in Charlotte Square, designed by Robert Adam though not completed by him. The former town house of the Duke of

Roxburghe is now one of Edinburgh's leading hotels. The Scottish Arts Council have their offices on the west side and the National Trust for Scotland occupy No. 5 on the south side. No. 6 is now the official residence of the Secretary of State for Scotland. No. 7 has been refurbished by the National Trust as a Georgian House with period furniture and fittings and is open to the public. The Moderator of the General Assembly of the Church of Scotland occupies the top floor.

Soon after its construction Princes Street began to change its character, the need for more shops squeezing out the residents into the later New Town development. Today, it is a jumble of conflicting styles, although such notable high Victorian buildings as Jenners (1893–95) by W. Hamilton Beattie and Forsyth's (1906–7) by Sir J. J. Burnet retain their confident excitement. Only the North British Hotel at the east end, Playfair's Royal Scottish Academy and National Gallery at the foot of The Mound and the Churches of St Cuthbert and St John at the west end, have been built on the south side of the street, so that the splendid and dominant position of the castle provides a unifying influence.

George Street has also become a shopping street. Rose Street, once renowned for other, less salubrious propensities, has recently been redeveloped, part of it as a pedestrian street, to create a new shopping centre. Even Thistle Street is acquiring a share of restaurants and boutiques.

Few private residents now live in the first New Town, which has become the domain of Edinburgh's lawyers (or Writers to the Signet as they are called) and other professional people. The largest scale later buildings tend to be banks, one of the most distinguished and grandest of which is No. 84, Sir J. J. Burnet's warehouse (1903–7), now restored for the National Westminster Bank.

The second phase of the New Town was begun in 1775, adding to the eastern approaches James Craig's St James's Square, now demolished to make way for the beetlingly aggressive and vulgarly over-assertive St James's Centre, housing an hotel and New St Andrew's House, the main centre of government administration in Scotland. York Place, developed by two builders, John Reid and John Young, has become somewhat dilapidated through long usage as office accommodation. Sir Henry Raeburn had his studio in No. 32. No. 5 was designed by James Adam. Alexander Nasmyth, the scenic painter responsible also for the most famous of all the portraits of Burns, lived in No. 47. In 1789, Nasmyth built the charming Doric temple St Bernard's Well in the wooded valley of the Water of Leith, which was eventually to become the New Town's own river. St Mary's Roman Catholic Cathedral, in Broughton Street, has a rebuilt Gothic elevation erected in 1814 by Gillespie Graham.

The third phase, usually referred to as 'the second New Town', was begun in 1803 to the north of Queen Street Gardens, with Dundas Street as its north/south axis. The architects Robert Reid and William Sibbald first put up Heriot Row. Northumberland Street, Abercromby Place and Jamaica Street followed, as well as William Playfair's Royal Circus, connecting with Drummond Place through Great King Street. The axis to the east continues through London Street, but lacks a terminal building. The splendid terraces, circuses and quadrants form the heart of the New Town residential area to this day and are remarkable for the rhythm of their fenestration and the liveliness of their co-ordinated detail. Notable in this phase is Thomas Brown's St Mary's Church, built in Bellevue Crescent in 1826.

The fourth phase, the building of the western approach to the New Town, was started in 1815, at about the same time as Regent Bridge and Waterloo Place were being constructed at the eastern end.

To the west, Melville Street, Alva Street, Lynedoch Place, part of Manor Place, Coates Crescent, Atholl Crescent and Maitland Street were built by 1830. Archibald Elliot's Rutland Square was built during the 1830s. Melville Street performs the function of axis to this section of the New Town, spaciously laid out. Its endpiece to the west, Sir Gilbert Scott's Gothic-style St Mary's Episcopal Cathedral, went up in 1879. Unfortunately, professional and commercial offices have displaced people in these grand but large-roomed houses, costly to heat now from the domestic purse.

The next extension to the New Town, Eglinton and Grosvenor Crescents, though dignified, feature the Victorian bay window, and mark off the western end of the great Georgian development.

Haymarket Station, built in 1842, was the original terminus of the railway from Glasgow, though four years later a tunnel had been drilled through the valley separating Old Town from New, and Waverley Station was established. Haymarket Station has been earmarked for redevelopment for more than a decade, but building-height restrictions imposed to preserve the dominating presence of Edinburgh Castle in the approaching perspectives led to the abandonment of massive high-rise proposals after considerable public agitation.

In the east, an ambitious addition around the Calton Hill area was begun in 1812. The Regent Bridge was flanked by the imposing Waterloo Place. Today, this is the area of the Post Office, of Old St Andrew's House (the work of Thomas S. Tait in 1939) and the cumbersome North British Hotel. On the vacant site down Leith Street from the restored Waterloo buildings the BBC promises one day to build a new headquarters for its Radio Scotland.

The original plans of 1812 by William Stark were not proceeded with, and it was Playfair who in 1819 carried out the major part of the scheme, notably Royal Terrace and Regent Terrace. The enclosed private gardens are thought to be the work of Joseph Paxton. Thomas Hamilton's Royal High School, one of Edinburgh's finest Greek revival buildings, was adapted internally in 1979 to house the Scottish Assembly. The failure of the Scots to achieve this through a referendum leaves Hamilton's building as a handsome monument to Scotland's traditional absence of self-confidence.

The monuments on Calton Hill are dominated by what looks like a colossal single-sided Parthenon. It was to have been a memorial church in honour of the Scots who fell in the Napoleonic wars. William Playfair designed it, George IV laid the foundation stone during his visit to Edinburgh in 1822, and work was begun two years later. After the construction of the twelfth column – each of them cost the then huge sum of one thousand pounds – the money ran out and, perhaps fortunately for the putative congregations, the work was stopped.

Playfair's monument (1832) to Dugald Stewart, Professor of Moral Philosophy at Edinburgh University and one of Burns's friends, and that to his uncle, the mathematician, John Playfair (1826) were, however, completed, as was the monument to Burns himself by Thomas Hamilton (1830). The decidedly non-Grecian monument to Nelson looks like an upended telescope and has a stone ball which is hoisted to the top and falls again when the one o'clock gun is fired from the Castle. The original City

Observatory (1776–92), designed by James Craig, is also a conspicuous landmark, as is the adjacent Observatory, the first building equipped with instruments to function as such, by W. H. Playfair (1818).

The sixth and final building phase of the New Town was begun in 1822, when James Gillespie Graham designed Ainslie Place, Moray Place, Albyn Place, Darnaway Street, Randolph Crescent and others on land feued by the 10th Earl of Moray. Moray Place has some of the grandest houses in Edinburgh's New Town, though today they are mostly divided into flats.

There was also some fairly substantial filling in. Stockbridge, feued by Sir Henry Raeburn when still an independent village, was developed and incorporated. William Playfair's St Stephen's Church (1827) is the district's most impressive public building. The Dean Village was also encompassed by the Georgian development. A little to the east of it, the charming Ann Street of 1816 is still one of Edinburgh's most expensive residential quarters. Telford's Dean Bridge of 1831 leads to Victorian crescents and terraces.

To the north east, Warriston Crescent, left unfinished in the 1820s, and Inverleith Row, near the beautifully laid out Royal Botanic Gardens, famous for its Rock Garden and its Plant House, opened in 1823, retain their Georgian dignity. Further east are Claremont Crescent, Hope Crescent, and Gayfield Square and the flats of Gayfield Place.

There were, of course, Georgian developments to the south of Edinburgh, notably in the South Bridge area reaching as far out as Newington. George Square preceded the first New Town. It was on this side of the City that in 1827 Playfair built the Old Quadrangle of Edinburgh University to altered plans by Robert Adam. The dome was an addition of 1887. The Upper Library Hall, now an art gallery and reception room, has magnificent proportions. The nearby MacEwan Hall dates from 1897. Now, of course, the University, founded in 1583 and the youngest of Scotland's mediaeval seats of learning, has departments in several areas of the modern city. The destruction of all but the west side of James Brown's George Square has enabled the University to expand near its original site. Buccleuch Place survives in University hands. From No. 18 in 1802, then the flat of Francis, later Lord Jeffrey, the *Edinburgh Review* was founded by a group that included the wit Sydney Smith and Henry (later Lord) Brougham.

The South Side of the city for long escaped the attentions of conservationists. Indeed, the New Town itself was gradually succumbing to a creeping development of offices from the south and the disease of slumdom from the north. Many of the poorer bits of Georgian Stockbridge were, in fact, demolished before the Civic Amenities Act of 1967 established the concept of the Conservation Area. In that year also The Scottish Civic Trust was founded. One of its first Trustees was the architect of London's New Zealand House and Royal Festival Hall, Sir Robert Matthew. Under his leadership, and with the co-operation of the Edinburgh Architectural Association (and at first rather more reluctant involvement of the then local authority, Edinburgh Corporation) The Scottish Civic Trust organised a rescue operation. This involved an unpaid professional and photographic survey of more than 5000 properties in the New Town, and an architectural and financial assessment of the findings and implications. An international conference was held under the chairmanship of Viscount Muirshiel, the Chairman of The Scottish Civic Trust, in June 1970, in a packed Assembly Rooms. The speakers included the Minister of State in the Scottish Office, Lord Hughes, the Lord Provost of Edinburgh, Wilson McKay, François Sorlin from France, Count Sforza from the Council of Europe, Sir Colin Buchanan and Sir John Betjeman. The Trust was charged with the setting up of a New Town Conservation Committee and regular financial support for a sustained restoration programme was promised by both central and local authorities. Edinburgh Corporation, from a position of apparent suspicion, swung in behind this energetic voluntary operation, and their successors after the reorganisation of local government in 1974/5, Edinburgh District, have honoured the original pledge, as have successive governments. The Edinburgh New Town Conservation Committee was set up in 1970 under the chairmanship of a former Lord Provost, Sir John Gregg Dunbar, with the architect Desmond Hodges as its first Director. Ten years after that founding conference, the long task of restitution of the properties making up this unique section of Edinburgh's European architectural heritage continues at a steady pace, though hampered to some extent by the inevitable restrictions and economic stringencies of world recession. The early history of this remarkable operation is to be found in *The Conservation of Georgian Edinburgh*, published by Edinburgh University Press.

In addition to the contrasting glories of its Old and New Towns, Edinburgh also possesses a heritage of buildings that enjoy their own individual distinction. As a centre of law and administration – the latter, albeit London-controlled since 1707 – it has established an educational tradition through schools such as George Heriot's, founded by James VI's goldsmith, nicknamed 'Jingling Geordie', and begun in 1528, four years after the benefactor's death. It was first used as a hospital on Cromwell's instructions after the Battle of Dunbar, but it settled into its academic function in 1659 and continues to do so to this day. It is a flamboyant building with towers at each quarter set round a quadrangle, rather like an Oxford college or the mediaeval university that Glasgow so unwisely destroyed in the 1870s. Robert Mylne added a dome-capped tower over its original northern entrance, and Playfair a cleverly imitative gateway when the main entrance was moved round to Lauriston Place. The statue of the founder is also Mylne's work.

Later schools, 'public' in the English sense of being privately financed outwith the state system and modelled more or less on Dr Arnold's Rugby, sprang up in the nineteenth century. They were housed in some outstanding and confident buildings. One of the most famous was founded by the banker Sir William Fettes. The grandiose turreted and ebulliently Victorian Franco-Scottish Gothic structure stands dominatingly north west of Stockbridge, and was put up by David Bryce between 1867–70. Daniel Stewart's, with its onion towers, was begun by David Rhind in 1849. The classical Edinburgh Academy, fee-paying but originally unendowed and founded by, among others, Sir Walter Scott and Lord Cockburn, is one of William Burn's most graceful works, in contrast to the much heavier John Watson's School at Belford, now in the process of conversion to become the National Gallery of Modern Art. George Watson's, now relocated at Myreside, once occupied a classical building by the Meadows at Lauriston, built on land feued from Heriot. In the category of large public buildings, west of Haymarket is the Tudor-Jacobean Donaldson's Hospital, a school for the deaf put up in 1842 to the bequest of John Donaldson, who died in 1830, and founded his school to educate the sons and daughters of the poor. W. H. Playfair was the architect.

A number of mansions that once stood in open country have now been engulfed by the City. Perhaps the most famous is Lauriston Castle, the home of John Law, whose financial wizardry for both the Scottish and the French governments collapsed, forcing him to flee to America, and leading him eventually to a poverty-stricken death in Venice. The Castle has a brilliantly successful Victorian addition by William Burn. Nearby is Caroline Park House (1696), its park now encroached upon by the suburb of Granton. Cramond House has at least the more congenial and less altered environment of the delightful village of Cramond, built in 1780–90 to house workers for mills on the River Almond, but now long since a residential suburb of the City. In spite of the achievements of its Georgian and Victorian builders, the twentieth century brought to Edinburgh the featureless spread and sprawl of bungaloid growth and council estates ranging from the indifferent to the visually (and sometimes socially and behaviourally) horrendous.

Stevenson was very rude indeed about the villas of the 1880s; but then he also complained of the New Town's 'draughty parallelograms', as did Southey earlier, complaining that 'the enormous length of the streets in the New Town' provided 'neither protection nor escape from the severe winds to which Edinburgh is exposed'. Stevenson did, however, catch something of the curious flavour of the place in words that, more than a century later, still carry the ring of truth: 'Edinburgh has but partly abdicated, and still wears, in parody, her metropolitan trappings. Half a capital and half a country town, the whole city leads a double existence; it has long trances of one and flashes of the other . . . it is half alive and half a monumental marble . . .'.

Scott's son-in-law, John Gibson Lockhart, caught in words another of the City's qualities almost 60 years earlier: 'Above all, here is all the sublimity of situation and scenery – mountains near and afar off – rocks and glens – and the sea itself, almost within hearing of the waves'.

Look down any of the sloping streets running north from George Street, and you catch a sudden sunlit glimpse of the Forth and the blue hills of Fife. To the south, the Pentlands are still very much to Edinburgh people Stevenson's 'hills of home'.

New buildings of distinction the City does possess, though they are not included in this pictorial survey, necessarily personal and therefore selective. Such outstanding contemporary buildings include the Commonwealth Swimming Pool and adjacent Scottish Widows building with its daring use of tinted glass, the Mortonhall Crematorium, several churches, among them Craigsbank Church and St John's Church Oxgangs, and private houses, notably 46A Dick Place, 1 Glenlockhart Bank and 'Avisfield' in Cramond Road North.

Banking, the direction of the law, and the business of government ensure that Edinburgh remains a going concern, unlike Glasgow, its larger and traditional 'rival' in the west, where the recession of its nineteenth-century industrial purpose has left it shrinking in a climate of economic decay.

Edinburgh has for several decades shared with Stratford-upon-Avon the distinction of being the United Kingdom's number two tourist attraction after London, a distinction consolidated by the success over more than 35 years of its International Festival of Music and the Arts. Unlike Salzburg, which has Mozart, or Munich, boasting Richard Strauss, Edinburgh offers a general cultural feast, its aim being always to attempt only the highest by international standards. As a by-product, many of its eating places have outgrown their traditional starchy Scots high-tea ambience to achieve European standards of cuisine.

The reputation for stand-offish aloofness with which its inhabitants have long been discredited – 'east-windy, west-endy', as the adage has it – is not wholly without foundation. Its ruling classes have been for successive generations the products of the professions rather than commerce. It has never really had to take off its fine clothes and sweat it out in the mines and shipyards and factories of once-grimy but also once-prosperous and now much-maligned Glasgow, with its fine Victorian architectural heritage.

What of Edinburgh's future? Banking, the administration of the law and the running of government seem likely to continue to flourish. Scotland, however, has been in the process of watering down its individuality, of diluting its sense of national purpose, for many generations now, and this process seems likely to continue. Yet Scotland – a greater beneficiary from European economic assistance than most of Britain – now seemingly combines a quite unhistoric dislike of Europe with a weary desire to be merged as painlessly as possible into the increasingly strident chauvinism of an apparently economically declining England. In circumstances such as these it is perhaps difficult to imagine a second Edinburgh 'Golden Age', either for the arts or their half-sister, architecture. At least, better late than never, we have learned to look after what we have inherited from a great and gracious past. The Capital of Scotland, 'half-abdicated' or not, remains one of the most beautiful cities of Europe, and, as Anthony Kersting's revealing photographs demonstrate, the possessor of a visual heritage by European standards as impressive as it is unique.

Bibliography

The City of Edinburgh: Royal Commission on Ancient Monuments, Scotland (HMSO, 1951)

The Conservation of Georgian Edinburgh (Edinburgh University Press, 1972)

Edinburgh: An Architectural Guide (The Edinburgh Architectural Association, 1969)

Wilmost Harrison, *Memorable Edinburgh Houses* (S. R. Publishers Ltd, 1971)

Maurice Lindsay, *The Lowlands of Scotland: Edinburgh and the South* (Robert Hale, 3rd edition, 1979)

Colin McWilliam, *Scottish Townscape* (Collins, 1975)

Ian Nimmo, *Portrait of Edinburgh* (Hale 1969)

Scottish Development Department List of Buildings of Special Architectural or Historical Interest

Sacheverell Sitwell and Francis Bamford, *Edinburgh* (John Lehmann, 1948)

A. J. Youngson, *The Making of Classical Edinburgh* (Edinburgh University Press, 1966)

Vistas and Views

Edinburgh is a hilly city, and therefore a city of vistas and views. The most spectacular are those from the Castle. As in Salzburg and Prague, a Castle dominates the city that has grown around it, over more than eight centuries. The waters of the Firth of Forth are never far away, and are glimpsed suddenly down hilly side streets as well as from vantage points. Beyond, the green fields in the Kingdom of Fife remind the burghers of Edinburgh that their city has never quite severed its links with the countryside.

1 The most familiar view of Edinburgh, showing the Castle, the Scott monument, the Royal Scottish Academy and, to the left, the National gallery. In the distance is the Caledonian Hotel and the spires of the St Mary's Episcopal Cathedral

23

2 *Left, above*   Princes Street, the long
downward hilly reach of the New Town
towards the Firth of Forth, and beyond, the
Kingdom of Fife, as seen from the Castle

3 *Left*   Looking west from the Castle
towards Corstorphine Hill with the spires of
St Mary's Cathedral in the middle distance

4 *Above*   A view of the battlements of the
Castle with Arthur's Seat in the
background. The stands in the Esplanade
are in the course of erection for the military
tattoo held annually during the Edinburgh
Festival. The spires are those of Tolbooth
St John's Church, St Giles and the old Tron
Kirk

5 An unusual vista from the Castle of the National Gallery, the Scott monument, the North British Hotel, the Calton Hill, and beyond, the Firth of Forth. The railway line into Waverley Station from the north and west passes under The Mound

6 Looking eastwards along Melville Street towards the West End from the roof of St Mary's Cathedral. The dome of the former St George's Church, Charlotte Square, now an extension of Register House, can be seen in the distance

7 The skyline of the Old Town from
Princes Street Gardens. On the left is the
headquarters of the Bank of Scotland
originally by Robert Reid and Richard
Crichton (1802–6), with alterations by
David Bryce (1865–70). The turreted towers
on the right are those of the gothic New
College by W. H. Playfair (1845–50)

The Old Town

The Old Town of Edinburgh reaches from the theatrical spectacle of Edinburgh Castle rock down the spine of the Royal Mile to the Palace of Holyroodhouse. Between these two buildings much of Scotland's history has been enacted, for in Parliament Square the laws of the country were passed, whilst St Giles has witnessed much of its stormy religious history. The mediaeval lands, or high tenements, reflect the days when Edinburgh was a walled city, and geographical considerations forced its citizens to build upwards. Neglect during the latter part of the nineteenth century and the earlier half of the twentieth has resulted in the loss of many of these historic buildings; but enough survive, especially between the Castlehill and the Lawnmarket and in the Canongate, to preserve something of the flavour of Edinburgh's mediaeval antiquity.

8 The Edinburgh skyline admired by the sculptured figures by Henry Moore in the Royal Botanic Gardens

9 *Far left* The Castle as seen from Castle Terrace. One of the many striking vistas of Edinburgh's oldest building

10 *Above* Another view of the Castle, this time from the much altered mediaeval Grassmarket

11 The Castle, from Johnston Terrace. In its present form the oldest part of the structure dates from the early eleventh century. The Esplanade, created between 1816 and 1820, is used annually for a military tattoo during the Edinburgh Festival, and temporary seating stands are erected to accommodate spectators

12 The modern entrance buildings to the Castle stand upon the inner wall and the defensive ditch. The statues of Sir William Wallace, the Guardian of Scotland, and its liberating king, Robert the Bruce, standing in niches on either side of the entrance, were unveiled in 1929. Two stone panels, probably of late sixteenth-century date and sculptured with a display of ordnance, are built into the walls of the arched entry. Since 1861, when the idea of a time-reminding gun was borrowed from the French, the one o'clock gun has been fired from the Half Moon Battery

13 *Right* King Robert the Bruce

14 *Far right* The Portcullis Gate was erected by the Regent Morton in 1574. It now contains a long vaulted trance which once had two outer double doors, a portcullis and an inner double door. Over this is the Portcullis Chamber

15 Foog's Gate, which gives entrance to the inner quarters of the Castle, including the Palace Yard, St Margaret's Chapel and the famous fifteenth-century cannon Mons Meg

16 St Margaret's Chapel, built around 1076 on the highest point of the Castle rock by Malcolm Canmore's wife, Queen Margaret. It holds only 26 worshippers

17 The chevroned chancel arch of St Margaret's Chapel

18 The Scottish National War Memorial designed by Sir Robert Lorimer and completed in 1927

19 The Scottish National War Memorial
Chapel

20 The Great Hall was built at the
beginning of the sixteenth century by
James IV and is noted for its timber
hammer-beam roof

21 The Castle Governor's House dates from 1742

22 *Right* The interior of the 'Highland Church'

23 *Far right* Looking down Castlehill with Tolbooth St John's Church, otherwise known as the 'Highland Church'. It was built by James Gillespie Graham between 1842–44 in collaboration with A. W. Pugin and has a decorated Gothic tower with pinnacles and an octagonal spire

24 Boswell's Court, 325 Castlehill, a seventeenth-century five-storey building with a moulded doorway and an inscription. It is named after a medical uncle of James Boswell, and was visited by Dr Johnson in the company of Boswell. Johnson spent his first night in Scotland in St James's Court, further down on the left

25 Cannonball House, on Castlehill, takes its name from the Jacobite cannon ball embedded in its west gable. Prince Charles Edward Stuart's forces captured most of eighteenth-century Edinburgh, but the Castle held out against him. The house has a crow-stepped gable to the south and was

built in 1630 by Alexander Mure, a furrier, who had his own initials and those of his wife inscribed in a dormer window facing west

26 Gladstone's Land, 483–489 Lawnmarket, was built between 1617 and 1620 by Thomas Gladstone, an ancestor of the future British Prime Minister. It has an arcaded ground-floor and six ashlared storeys. It also has an outside stair. Inside are painted ceilings, probably the work of Italian craftsmen, and original fireplaces. The property of the National Trust for Scotland and a period museum, it was restored in 1935 by Sir Frank Mears and again in 1979–80

27 The principal room in Gladstone's Land as it was seen by visitors to the Saltire Society from 1936 to 1978

28 *Right* Mylne's Court, 513–523 Lawnmarket, is the earliest attempt at open planning in the Old Town. Unfortunately the west and part of the east side have been demolished, but the north block and the street front of six floors, dated 1619, and the work of Robert Mylne, the architect of much of the work at Holyroodhouse, remain. They were restored by Ian Lindsay & Partners in 1968 as a hall of residence for Edinburgh University

29 *Far right* Lady Stair's House, behind Gladstone's Land, in Lady Stair's Close. Now used as a City museum, it houses relics relating to Burns, Scott and Stevenson. In the dining-hall there is a musicians' gallery and a turnpike stair. Eleanor, Countess Dowager of Stair, formerly Lady Primrose, inspired Sir Walter Scott's story *My Aunt Margaret's Mirror*. In Lady Stair's day terraced gardens descended from the house to the shores of the Nor' Loch. It was extensively and badly restored in the nineteenth century

30 *Left*   Looking up the West Bow of the
mediaeval Grassmarket, an area which
suffered from improvements made in 1840,
and has been badly affected by further
demolitions in the mid-twentieth century

31 *Above*   The West Bow, looking down
to the Grassmarket

32 Candlemakers' Hall, at the head of Candlemaker Row which leads up from the Grassmarket to the south, is a fine eighteenth-century building with two towers, dated 1722. Restored, it is now the home of the Edinburgh Press Club

33 and 34 Ramsay Gardens, built round the house of Allan Ramsay, the portrait painter, designed for his father, Allan Ramsay the poet, has nineteenth-century additions and alterations, romantically conceived by Sir Patrick Geddes (whose Outlook Tower Building is nearby) and carried out in 1893 by the architect Henbest Capper

48

35 *Far left*   The
Tron Kirk from the
north west, founded
in 1633, designed by
John Mylne. It was
badly damaged in
the great fire of 1824
and the present
steeple was
thereafter designed
by R. & R. Dickson
in 1828.
Edinburgh's public
weighing beam or
tron once stood
outside the church

36 *Left, above*
Parliament Square,
with the High Kirk
of St Giles on
the left and the City
Chambers in the
background

37 The City
Chambers, 249 High
Street, was built
between 1753 and
1761 as a Royal
Exchange by the
architect John
Fergus to designs by
John Adam. It has
long since been used
as the meeting place
for the Town
Council, now
Edinburgh District
Council, and has
been considerably
altered and adapted
for this purpose.
The rear elevation,
eleven storeys high,
is one of the tallest
buildings that
remain in the Old
Town

38 Parliament Hall was built between 1632 and 1639 to house the Scottish Parliament. The original exterior has been covered by later additions, including the Law Courts and the Signet Library, and a façade built in 1808 by the architect Robert Reid. Inside, Parliament Hall, 122 feet in length, still has its original seventeenth-century timber roof

39 *Right*   The fine statue of Henry Dundas, Viscount Melville, in Parliament Hall, by Sir Francis Chantrey

40 *Far right*   The magnificent open roof ceiling of the Parliament Hall was constructed *circa* 1640 by John Scott, master wright, mainly of oaks grown at Culross and Balgonie in Fife

41 The Signet Library in Parliament House, lined with Corinthian columns and lit by a central saucer dome, the work of William Stark (1770–1813)

42 *Right* A detail of the dome in the Signet Library

43 *Far right* The Mercat Cross. The shaft is from the original sixteenth-century Cross, but the replica octagonal base and platform, though traditional in design, date from 1885. They were presented by W. E. Gladstone. This is the point in Edinburgh from which Royal proclamations are made. The Mercat Cross was heavily restored in 1970

44 *Above* The High Kirk of St Giles, viewed from the west. St Giles was originally Edinburgh's only parish church, but became a cathedral when the Diocese of Edinburgh was founded in 1633 by Charles I

45 *Right* The crowned tower of St Giles, dating from 1500. It was the only part of the building to escape the unfortunate refacing with paving stones by William Burn in 1829

46 *Far right* St Giles, seen from Parliament Square. The equestrian statue of Charles II is in the foreground

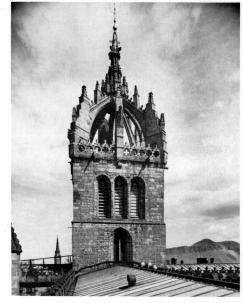

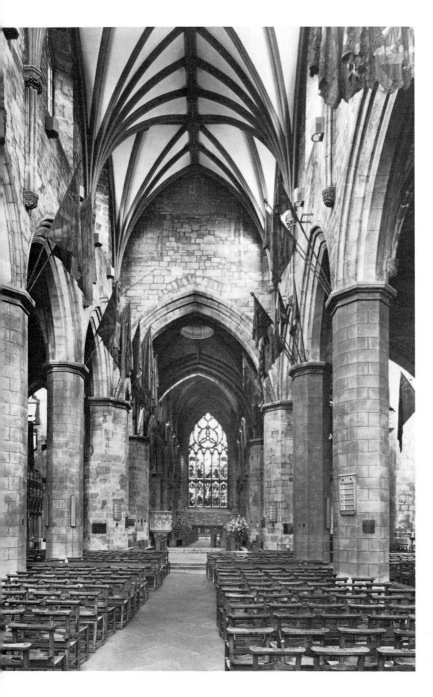

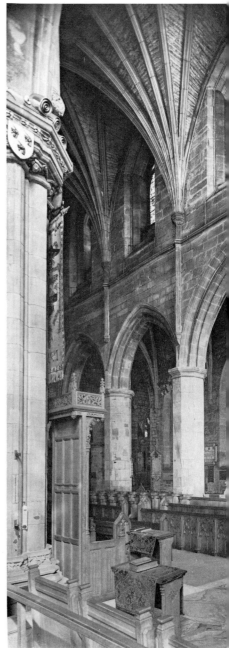

47 The nave of the High Kirk of St Giles

48 The north side of the choir added about 1460

49 The Chapel of the Most Ancient and Most Noble Order of the Thistle, the latest addition to St Giles, was designed by Sir Robert Lorimer in 1910

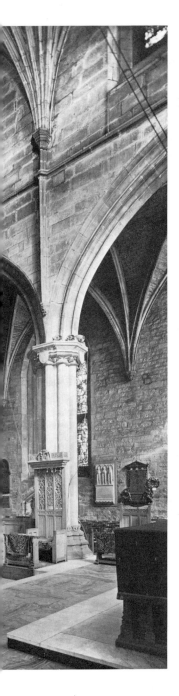

50 *Left*   The Thistle Chapel, facing west

51 *Above, left*   The Royal Pew of the Thistle Chapel

52 *Above, right*   A musical angel on the roof of the Thistle Chapel

53 The statue of John Knox by Pittendrigh MacGillivray. It stood inside St Giles when this photograph was taken, but now weathers in Parliament Square

54 *Above* A detail of the monument in St Giles to the 8th Earl and 1st Marquess of Argyle, beheaded in 1661

55 *Right* The only extant equestrian statue in Great Britain to Charles II. The designer is now unknown. It was cast in lead in 1685, and stands almost over the burial place of the Reformer John Knox

56 *Far right* The Magdalen Chapel, 39 Cowgate, was founded in 1541. Its tower was built in 1618, the street frontage in 1857

57 and 58 The interior of the Magdalen Chapel, which contains the only Scottish mediaeval example of stained glass surviving in its original building. Renovation work on the Chapel was instituted by George Hay in 1960

59 The Tolbooth, 163 Canongate. Canongate was at one time a separate burgh and the Tolbooth of 1592 was its civic centre. The turreted steeple is characteristic of the period, although the clock is Victorian, part of the restoration of 1879

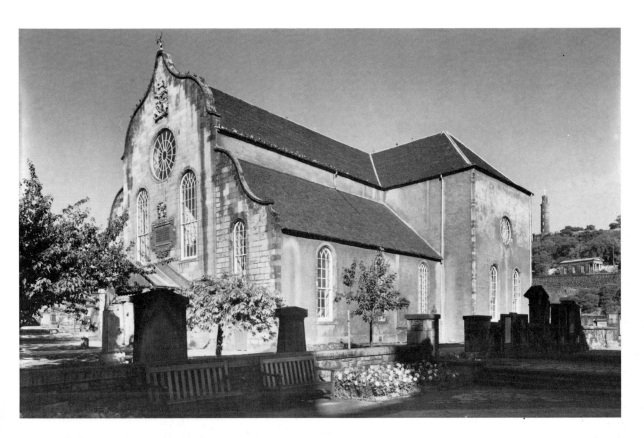

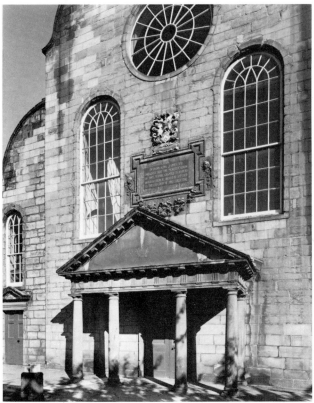

60 *Far left* John Knox's House. The only surviving timber galleried house in the High Street, credited by legend with being at one time the home of John Knox. There is no evidence to suggest that it was in fact the Reformer's house, but the tradition has been responsible for its survival. In 1849 it was condemned as a ruinous fabric but following representations at that time repairs were carried out to the sixteenth-century building

61 *Above* Canongate Church, surrounded by its churchyard. The Church was designed in 1688 by James Smith for the congregation displaced by King James VII and II when he converted the Abbey Church of Holyroodhouse into a chapel for his newly revived order of Knights of the Thistle. The churchyard contains many memorial stones, including that erected by Robert Burns over the grave of his predecessor, the Edinburgh poet Robert Fergusson

62 The entrance to Canongate Church

63 Looking up Canongate

64 Huntly House Museum, 149 Canongate,
its upper floors of projecting timber
construction and plastered. Dated 1570, it
has a Latin inscription in replica, the
original now being preserved in a museum.
It is now a City Museum, and contains relics
from demolished houses. Its restoration was
carried out by Sir Frank Mears

65 Another view up Canongate

66 *Left, above* White Horse Close, 31
Canongate. The seventeenth-century White
Horse Inn was restored in 1889 and again in
1964

67 *Left* A detail of the modern housing,
from the latest restoration of the White
Horse Inn in Canongate

68 *Above* The west front of the Palace of
Holyroodhouse from the south west. The
north west tower is early sixteenth century,
the remainder designed by Sir William
Bruce, but carried out by Robert Mylne, the
King's Master Mason 1671–79

69 The entrance to the Palace of Holyroodhouse, at the foot of the Royal Mile. When the Canongate was a separate burgh, debtors could find a refuge from arrest in the Abbey sanctuary

70 *Right, above* The Palace of Holyroodhouse seen through the Palace Yard gates, designed by Sir George Washington Browne and erected as a memorial to Edward VII

71 The Abbey of Holyrood, founded by David I in 1128 though much is later

72 The west archway of Holyrood Abbey

The New Town

It is in a sense wrong to speak of Edinburgh New Town, because in fact the area so designated – the largest and best unified example of eighteenth- and early nineteenth-century classical town planning in Europe – was built in seven stages, and these are distinguished in the photographs that follow. Edinburgh's great Lord Provost George Drummond felt that at a time when military threat seemed improbable, the population was growing and prosperity and fame were increasing, the constricted life of the Old Town on the rock had become intolerable. He therefore persuaded the Town Council to encourage expansion to the north, after a tentative move in the direction of George Square. In their way was the Nor' Loch, a large but marshy sheet of water immediately below the Castle and the Old Town, where Princes Street Gardens lie today. Lord Provost Drummond and his Town Council drained the marsh and threw the North Bridge over the marshy land to the east of it. The Mound was a later link.

The design of the New Town was open to competition, and James Craig's prize-winning plan of 1768, slightly modified, began the work of transformation.

Soon there was a 'flitting' (as moving house is described in Scotland), amongst the first to move being the philosopher and well-known sceptic David Hume, a female wag adding the name 'saint' to David Street, named in his honour. By the time the New Town had merged into the Victorian terraces – in turn to merge with villa suburban development and, later, less architecturally happy development in our own century – the Old Town had started to degenerate into that slumdom which was to remain its fate until the concept of conservation became accepted in the second half of the present century. The New Town also began to degenerate, commercial development eating into Princes Street soon after it was completed, taking over George Street, invading Queen Street and even threatening the grander domestic crescents and terraces to the north. Fortunately, the creation of Conservation Areas, arising out of the 1967 Civic Amenities Act and now incorporated in Scotland's planning laws, halted this development. The Scottish Civic Trust's international conference of 1970, leading to the founding of the Edinburgh New Town Conservation Committee financed by both Central Government and Local Authority, began the slow, but, let us hope, permanent reversal of the New Town's fortunes.

First Phase (1768)

73 *Left, above* Register House, begun in
1774 to the design of Robert Adam to house
the national records and in use by 1778,
after delays due to lack of money. Robert
Reid, the last of the King's Master Masons,
altered Adam's plans when completing it in
1822

74 *Left* The equestrian statue of the Duke
of Wellington outside Register House was
completed by Sir John Steele in 1852 to
commemorate the anniversary of Waterloo

75 *Above* Jenners store in Princes Street,
designed by Sir William Hamilton Beattie in
1895. He was also the architect of the North
British Hotel, built for the railway company
of which Jenner was chairman

76 *Far left* Forsyths Building in Princes Street, now several shops, was built in 1909, Edinburgh's first steel-framed building. Like Jenner's, Forsyths replaced simple Georgian buildings which were amongst the earliest of the first New Town

77 *Left* The monument in Princes Street to Sir Walter Scott, completed in 1844 to the design of G. M. Kemp, who won an open architectural competition. The statue of Scott within the monument is by Sir John Steele, and was added two years later

78 *Below* The Royal Scottish Academy was designed by William Henry Playfair in 1823 and enlarged by him in 1836. Sir John Steele designed the statue of Queen Victoria over the portico. In the foreground is the National Gallery, another of Playfair's masterpieces dating from 1845. During the late 1970s a most skilful and almost imperceptible modern addition was made beneath and to the north side of the building

79 *Left, above* Playfair's façade of the
National Gallery

80 *Left* A glimpse of two of the galleries
in the National Gallery of Scotland

81 *Above* The handsome headquarters of
the Bank of Scotland on The Mound, built
by Robert Reid and Richard Crichton in
1806, but much altered by David Bryce in
1870

82 Edinburgh's principal concert hall, the
Usher Hall in Lothian Road, designed by
Stockdale Harrison in 1910

83 The monument in St Andrew Square to
Henry Dundas, 1st Viscount Melville, was
designed by William Burn in 1821. The
statue is by Robert Forrest, and dates from
1828

84 St John's Episcopal Church, at the West
End of Princes Street, designed by William
Burn in 1816

85 *Left* The spacious interior of St John's Episcopal Church

86 *Above* St Cuthbert's Church, surrounded by its churchyard, at the West End of Princes Street, most picturesquely situated, has a steeple dating from 1789 and attributed to the architect H. Weir. The steeple is the only part of the original church retained in the design of the present building of 1894 by Hippolyte J. Blanc

87 *Far left* No. 26 St Andrew Square, designed by Sir William Chambers (1770–72)

88 *Left* No. 35 St Andrew Square, designed in 1796 by Sir William Chambers

89 The Royal Bank of Scotland, St Andrew Square, designed by Sir William Chambers (1772–74) as a house for Sir Laurence Dundas

90 *Right* In the foreground of the Royal Bank of Scotland is the Hopetoun Monument. The equestrian statue of John Hope, 4th Earl of Hopetoun, is by Thomas Campbell and was erected around 1830. It has an inscription by Sir Walter Scott

91 *Below* The Bank of Scotland, St Andrew Square

92 *Far right* No 39 St Andrew Square, designed by David Bryce for the British Linen Bank, 1851–52, now part of the Bank of Scotland

87

93 The Royal Bank of Scotland, 14 George
Street, designed by David Rhind in 1847.
The decorative frontal fresco, or sculptured
pediment, is by A. Handyside Ritchie

94 The Clydesdale Bank, 29–31 George Street, designed by David Bryce in 1847

95 The handsome Standard Life Assurance Building in George Street by J. M. Dick Peddie (1897–1901). Beyond is St Andrew's Church, the work of Major Andrew Frazer of the Royal Engineers, designed in 1781, and executed 1782–84, with a spire designed by William Sibbald in 1789

96 *Far left* St Andrew's Church, Major Frazer's only known masterpiece, indeed his only known building

97 *Above* Looking north along George Street, with the George Hotel, St Andrew's Church and, in the distance, the Melville Monument

98 The statue of George IV in George Street by Sir Francis Chantrey, erected in 1831

99 *Left, above*   The beautiful Assembly
Rooms designed by John Henderson, and
built by public subscription, 1784–87. In the
gracious first floor hall, Sir Walter Scott first
publicly admitted to being the author of the
Waverley Novels. An imposing but heavier
addition behind is the Music Hall of
William Burn, 1818–24

100 *Left*   No. 39 North Castle Street,
completed in 1790 and the town house of
Sir Walter Scott from 1802 to 1826

101 *Above*   101–103 George Street, The
Bank of Scotland, designed by J. M. Dick
Peddie, 1883–85

102 *Left, above* Charlotte Square was
designed by Robert Adam in 1791 but only
the north side, illustrated here, was
completed in 1793. The remainder of the
Square was realised by Robert Reid in 1815

103 *Left* The centrepiece of the north side
of Charlotte Square

104 The Scottish National Portrait Gallery
in Queen Street, designed by Sir R. Rowand
Anderson in 1890. The sculpture is by
Birnie Rhind

105 *Left*   The impressive façade of No. 9
Queen Street, the Royal College of
Physicians

106 *Above*   Albyn Place, the work of
James Gillespie Graham, 1822

Second Phase (1775)

107 *Right* No. 32 York Place, completed in 1795, was Sir Henry Raeburn's studio 1798–1809

108 *Below* St Paul's Episcopal Church, York Place, designed by Archibald Elliott, 1816–1818

109 *Far right* St Bernard's Well, designed by Alexander Nasmyth, the architect and painter, in 1789. It was restored in 1888 by Thomas Bonnar. The statue of Hygeia was designed by D. W. Stevenson in 1888

Third Phase (1802)

110 *Left, above* Heriot Row, designed by
Robert Reid and William Sibbald. Work
was begun in 1802

111 *Left* No. 17 Heriot Row, the
boyhood home of R. L. Stevenson

112 *Above* Another of the splendid
domestic ranges of Reid and Sibbald,
Abercromby Place, dating from 1804

113 *Left, above* Northumberland Street,
again by Reid and Sibbald, put up in 1811.
It had begun to decline prior to the work of
restoration following the Scottish Civic
Trust's New Town Conference in 1970

114 *Left* Great King Street, the feuing
plan for which is dated 1810. Reid and
Sibbald designed this street as symmetrical
blocks

115 *Above* India Street, designed by Reid
and Sibbald and begun in 1819

116 London Street, begun in 1806 and another of Reid and Sibbald's streets, rudely called by Stevenson 'drafty parallelograms'

117 and 118 Drummond Place, begun by Reid and Sibbald in 1804 and finished in 1823. Most of these splendid houses were originally single homes, although the majority are now skilfully sub-divided into flats

119 Royal Circus, the work of William Henry Playfair, who designed the elevations. It was, however, completed by Reid and Sibbald in 1823

120 and 121 St Mary's Church, Bellevue Crescent, the work of Thomas Brown, 1826. Bellevue Crescent was begun by Reid and Sibbald in 1802, and completed in 1869

Fourth Phase
(1815)

122 *Left, above*   Regent's Bridge, designed
by Archibald Elliott in 1815 as a war
memorial. It consists of Ionic screens with a
Corinthian arch in the middle

123 *Left*   Waterloo Place, designed by
Archibald Elliott in 1815 and recently
restored

124 *Above*   A slightly later development at
the other end of the New Town, Alva Street
by James Gillespie Graham, dating from
1826

125 Rutland Square, also by Archibald Elliott, designed in 1819 but built by John Tait between 1830 and 1840. No. 15 now houses the headquarters of the Royal Incorporation of Architects in Scotland

126 The east side of Rutland Square and Rutland Street

127 Melville Street, named after Henry Dundas, the 1st Viscount Melville, was designed by Robert Brown in 1814 and built between 1820 and 1826

128 Melville Crescent, the work of John Lessels, 1855–56

129 Atholl Crescent, one of two crescents gracing the approach to the New Town from Glasgow, is by Thomas Bonnar, and was built in 1824–25

130 St George's
West Church by
David Bryce, 1869.
It has a campanile
added by Sir R.
Rowand Anderson
in 1879

131 Coates
Crescent, opposite
Atholl Crescent, was
built between
1813 and 1823. The
name of the architect
is uncertain

132 Melville Street,
looking towards St
Mary's Cathedral.
The memorial by Sir
John Steele to
Viscount Melville
dates from 1857

133 No. 25 Melville Street, designed by Robert Brown in 1814 and built 1820–26

134 *Left* The Cathedral Church of St Mary was built for the Episcopalian Church by Sir George Gilbert Scott in 1879. Its cluster of spires forms one of the dominating punctuation marks in the centre of the Edinburgh landscape

135 St Mary's Cathedral from the west

136 *Far left*   The nave of St Mary's Cathedral facing east

137 *Left*   St Mary's Cathedral, the Bishop's Throne

138 Frank Brangwyn's mural in the Song School of St Mary's Cathedral

139 and 140 Old or Easter Coates House, dating from 1615. It now houses the St Mary's School of Music for specially gifted children

Fifth Phase (1819)

141 William Henry Playfair's Observatory on Calton Hill, designed in 1818. Its establishment was largely due to his uncle, Professor John Playfair, who had recently become president of the newly formed Astronomical Institution

142 *Right* Observatory House and the monument to Dugald Stewart on Calton Hill. Dugald Steward, the Professor of Moral Philosophy at Edinburgh University, owned Catrine House, Ayrshire, and was a friend of Robert Burns. W. H. Playfair designed this monument in 1832

143 *Far right* Looking westwards over Edinburgh from Dugald Stewart's monument on Calton Hill

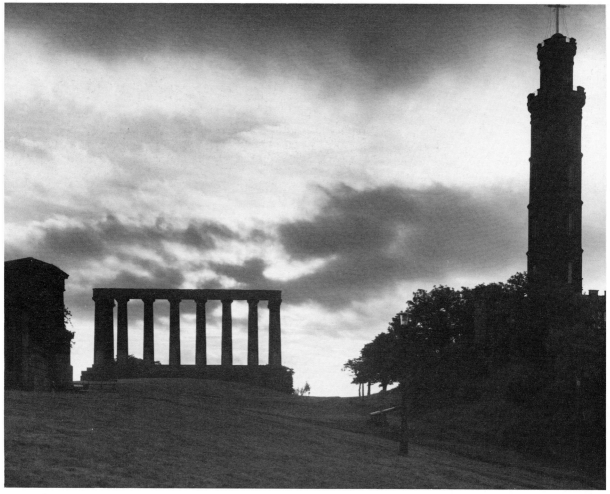

144 *Left, above*   Observatory House,
Calton Hill, begun in 1776 as an
observatory by James Craig, finished in
1792, but never properly equipped with
astronomical instruments

145 *Left*   Sunrise on the Calton Hill. In the
centre is the National Monument, intended
to be a replica of the Parthenon and to
commemorate the dead in the Napoleonic
wars. The foundation stone was laid in
August 1822, during George IV's visit to
Edinburgh. The design was by W. H.

Playfair and C. R. Cockerell, but the church
was never completed, the money running
out after the erection of the 12 columns. To
the right is Nelson's monument, designed
shortly after Trafalgar by Robert Burn,
whom the poet Burns employed to put a
headstone over the grave of Robert
Fergusson in the Canongate Church. The
Nelson monument was completed by R. &
D. Dickson in 1816

146 *Above*   The impressive pillars of the
National Monument on Calton Hill

147 *Left* The circular monument on Calton Hill to the philosopher David Hume, designed by Robert Adam in 1777

148 *Above* W. H. Playfair's monument to his uncle, the great mathematician and natural philosopher John Playfair, designed in 1826

149 *Above right* The monument to Robert Burns by Thomas Hamilton, a circular Greek temple completed in 1830

150 Thomas Hamilton's Royal High
School, on the face of Calton Hill, designed
in 1829. It was adapted internally for the
proposed Scottish Assembly in 1978–79

151 Calton Old Burial Ground, which
contains many interesting monuments,
including that to Hume, on the left, and the
obelisk designed in 1844 by Thomas
Hamilton to commemorate the Political
Martyrs of 1793. Also in the picture is the
Governor's House for the Old Calton Jail,
designed by Archibald Elliott in 1815. With
the same sort of unconsciously humorous
irony that led Edinburgh to place the statue
of Charles II almost on top of John Knox's
bones, the Old Calton Jail was demolished
in the 1930s to make way for the then seat
of government in Scotland, St Andrew's
House

152 Royal Terrace, designed in 1821–24 by
W. H. Playfair but not completed until
1860. It has a communal garden at the rear
laid out by Sir Joseph Paxton

153 Typical New Town railings and lamps, now being reproduced in replica. These examples are in Royal Terrace

154 Regent Terrace designed by W. H. Playfair in 1825

155 Calton Terrace, designed by W. H. Playfair, was completed in 1860, though designed some 40 years before and shares the communal garden laid out by Sir Joseph Paxton for Regent Terrace and Royal Terrace

156 and 157 Nos. 1–5 and 6–10 Blenheim Place, designed by the industrious W. H. Playfair in 1819, who also designed Regent Terrace Place (154). There have been various conversions for commercial uses in our times

Sixth Phase (1822)

The Moray Estate was feued by the 10th Earl of Moray as individual houses, and James Gillespie Graham was commissioned to design the lay-out in 1822. It consisted of a crescent, an oval and a polygon, linked by new streets to the earlier development

158 *Far left*
Randolph
Crescent is part of
this development

159 and
160 Randolph
Place, begun in 1810
but not completed
until 1826, along
with Randolph Cliff

161 *Left* Moray Place, among the
grandest ranges in the New Town, though
considered by some to be rather heavily
ornate

162 *Above* Darnaway Street, another
development of the Moray Estate and the
work of James Gillespie Graham

163 St Bernard's Crescent, built at about the same time, was designed by James Milne in 1824

164 Upper Dean Terrace designed by James Milne in 1824

165 *Right* Danube Street designed by
James Milne in 1824

166 *Below* Dean Terrace designed in 1824
by James Milne

167 *Far right* Belgrave Crescent, by far
the most imposing of the Victorian terraces
which continued the discipline of Georgian
Edinburgh at the West End, and the work
of John Chesser, 1874

168 In marked contrast, The Colonies, Glenogle Road, consist of ten parallel two-storey terraces with access to upper floors by outside stairs. They were built in 1861 by the Edinburgh Co-operative Building Company, and are the most extensive of several such schemes

Fringe Developments

169 The spectacular St Stephen's Church. Entering by the front door, the visitor arrives in the gallery. It is the work of W. H. Playfair, dating from 1827, though later altered internally

170 *Left* Well Court in the Dean Village. Originally called the Water of Leith Village, the Dean Village was once the site of the flour mills that supplied Edinburgh. Until Telford's Dean Bridge was erected in 1832, travellers to Queensferry crossed the Water of Leith here. The Village, now mainly owned by the Local Authority, has been in part reconstructed for housing

171 *Above* Well Court, the construction of which was originally envisaged by John R. Findlay, a member of the family who owned *The Scotsman* newspaper until it was taken over by the Thomson Organisation

172 The reconstructed Old Tolbooth in the Dean Village

173 The doorway of the Old Tolbooth

174 The Water of Leith flowing through Dean Village. The church beside Dean Bridge is the former Holy Trinity Episcopal Church of 1838 by John Henderson, now an electricity transformer station

175 *Left, above* Dean Bridge erected by the engineer Thomas Telford in 1832

176 *Left* The charming Ann Street, one of the most exclusive residential streets in the New Town, was speculatively conceived in two sections by Sir Henry Raeburn. The first part was completed in 1825, and the second in 1869–70

177 Off Leith Walk, Gayfield Place and Gayfield Square, of which this is No. 33, were built by James Begg in 1791, at that time very much on the northern periphery

The South Side

178 *Left* Surgeons Hall, Nicolson Street, was completed in 1832 and is the work of W. H. Playfair. It was restored by Robert Hurd & Partners in the late 1950s

179 *Above* The Royal Archers' Hall, Buccleuch Street, was built in 1776. The original architect is unknown, but the additional section is the work of Sir R. Rowand Anderson. It is the headquarters of the Queen's Bodyguard in Scotland, the Royal Company of Archers

180, 181 and 182 The Royal Scottish
Museum, Chambers Street, was designed in
1861 by Captain Fowke of the Royal
Engineers. It is remarkable internally for its
use of structural cast iron, both in the
stairways and the balconies

183 George Heriot's Hospital, begun in
1628 following a bequest from Heriot,
goldsmith to James VI. The school was
begun by William Wallace, the King's
Master mason, and completed by his
successor William Ayton, though Robert
Mylne added the domed clock tower in
1693. It appears that a 'paterne' for the
design was supplied by Dr Balcanquhal,
Dean of Rochester

184 Robert Mylne's clock tower

185 The Heriot-Watt University building at 23 Chambers Street, a free Renaissance Victorian composition by John Chesser, 1886–88. To the right of the central pavilion is David Rhind's Watt Institution of 1872. On the left, the former Phrenological Museum by David Cousin, 1775–77. The Watt Institution was so named in 1851, incorporating the School of Arts of 1821 founded by Leonard Horner. The Chesser central pavilion is flanked by busts of Horner to the right and to the left of George Heriot, out of whose educational endowments commission the Watt Institution was built

186 The main entrance to the Old College, the University of Edinburgh. The original design was by Robert Adam, dating from 1782. Only the street frontage of this scheme was completed. The continuations were by W. H. Playfair in 1834 and the dome was the work of Sir R. Rowand Anderson designed about 1880, and larger than that originally intended by Adam

187 The courtyard and dome of Edinburgh University

188 The McEwan Hall, built in 1897 for Edinburgh University by Sir R. Rowand Anderson. Its uses for the performance of music are somewhat limited because of its lengthy echo

189 The west and only surviving side of George Square. The complete square was speculatively built by James Brown in 1763–64 and was the first residential unit outside the Old Town. Unfortunately, three-quarters of the Square have been demolished to make way for extensions to Edinburgh University, the design of most of the new buildings being by no means universally admired

190 and 191 Greyfriars Church is of considerable historical significance. The eastern part is dated 1620 and the National Covenant was signed in it in 1638. An additional church was built on to the west end in 1722 by Alexander McGill. Both were formed into one church in 1938 after restoration by H. F. Kerr. The churchyard is the burial place of the Adam family of architects. There is a statue of a dog, Greyfriars Bobby, on the pavement outside, much beloved by tourists

192 Blacket Place, a housing scheme, grouped behind lodges and gates which were closed at night. It is the work of James Gillespie Graham, completed around 1860

Peripheral Public Buildings

193 One of Edinburgh's many ebullient
Victorian schools, Fettes College, built with
money donated by the banker Sir William
Fettes by David Bryce between 1864 and
1870 in a richly decorative Franco-Scottish
Gothic style

194 Fettes College, the modern Dining Hall

195 and 196 Daniel Stewart's College by
David Rhind, built between 1849 and 1855
in a neo-Jacobean style

197 *Left, above*   The Dean Orphanage
designed by Thomas Hamilton in 1883

198 *Left*   Hamilton's portico to the Dean
Orphanage

199 *Above*   Donaldson's Hospital by
W. H. Playfair, built between 1842–54,
Tudor Jacobean in style, and now a School
for the Deaf

200 *Far left*　A detail of the front elevation of Donaldson's Hospital

201 *Above*　John Watson's School, built by William Burn in 1825, now houses the National Gallery of Modern Art

202 The portico of Burn's John Watson's School

203 *Left, above* Edinburgh Academy, also the work of William Burn, built between 1823 and 1836

204 *Left* St Andrew's House, until the removal to New St Andrew's House in the St James Centre at the head of Leith Walk, the centre of government administration in Scotland. Built on the site of the old Calton Jail, it was completed in 1939 by Thomas S. Tait

205 *Above* An Edinburgh curiosity. The sixteenth-century Dovecot in Dovecot Road. It is in the grounds of Edinburgh Tapestry Company Dovecot Studios, established in 1912

206 The Royal Botanic Gardens Large Palm House by Robert Mathieson built in 1858. There is a spectacular modern addition designed by G. A. H. Pearce and opened in 1967

207 The Barclay Church, designed by F. T. Pilkington and put up in 1862–64. It has an interesting heart- and trefoil-shaped auditorium

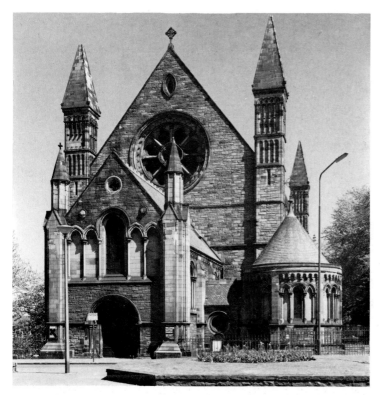

208 *Far left* St Ninian's, on the corner of St John's Road and St Ninian's Road, was originally built in 1844–5 as a simple plain structure for the Free Church. In 1869 it was embellished and given a new front in a kind of French Gothic style. The north apse for the organ and pulpit was added in 1889, and between 1911–14 the transepts were put on

209 *Left* The former Catholic Apostolic Church, Mansfield Place, now Bellevue Baptist Church, was designed by Sir R. Rowand Anderson, begun in 1873 and completed to a revised design in 1894

210 Cramond Village, built between 1780 and 1790, was designed to house the workers for mills operating on the River Almond. It has long since become an exclusive residential suburb of Edinburgh. Restoration work was carried out in 1961 by Ian G. Lindsay & Partners for Edinburgh Corporation

211 The early sixteenth-century Cramond
Old Bridge was rebuilt in 1619, and has
since been further repaired, although not to
the detriment of its original character.

212 Cramond Parish Church dates from
1656, with an older fifteenth-century tower.
The church was extended and altered in
1701, and again by Robert Burn in 1811.
Further repairs and alterations were carried
out by William Burn 1828, Robert Bell
1843, David Bryce 1851, 1863 and a large
reconstruction took place in 1911–12 by
David McArthy and James Mather. There is
a fine collection of tombstones

213 Cramond House dates from 1680, when the two-storey and basement central part was built for John Inglis. Mid-eighteenth-century remodelling was carried out for Sir John Inglis

214 Murrayfield House was built about 1735 for Archibald Murray, the wing being added around 1780

215 Dalry House, Orwell Place, a mid-seventeenth-century country house with a polygonal stair tower repeated on an early nineteenth-century extension. It was restored in 1965 as an old people's Day Centre by Robert Hurd & Partners

216 *Far left* Prestonfield House represents the rebuilding in 1687 of an older house. The architect was Sir William Bruce. It is at present an hotel

217 *Left* Inverleith House was built in 1774 by David Henderson. Alterations were made in 1877 and again in our day

218 The Stenhouse Mansion, a private residence built in 1623, was restored in 1964 for the National Trust for Scotland by Ian G. Lindsay and Partners and is now used as fine art conservation studios

219 Caroline Park Mansion dates from 1696

220 and 221 Lauriston Castle was built by Sir Archibald Napier of Merchiston in the sixteenth century. It has alterations by William Burn made in the nineteenth century

222 A range of buildings in Merchiston Castle
School, designed by W. J. Walker Todd in
1929. The school is based on the early
nineteenth-century Colinton House

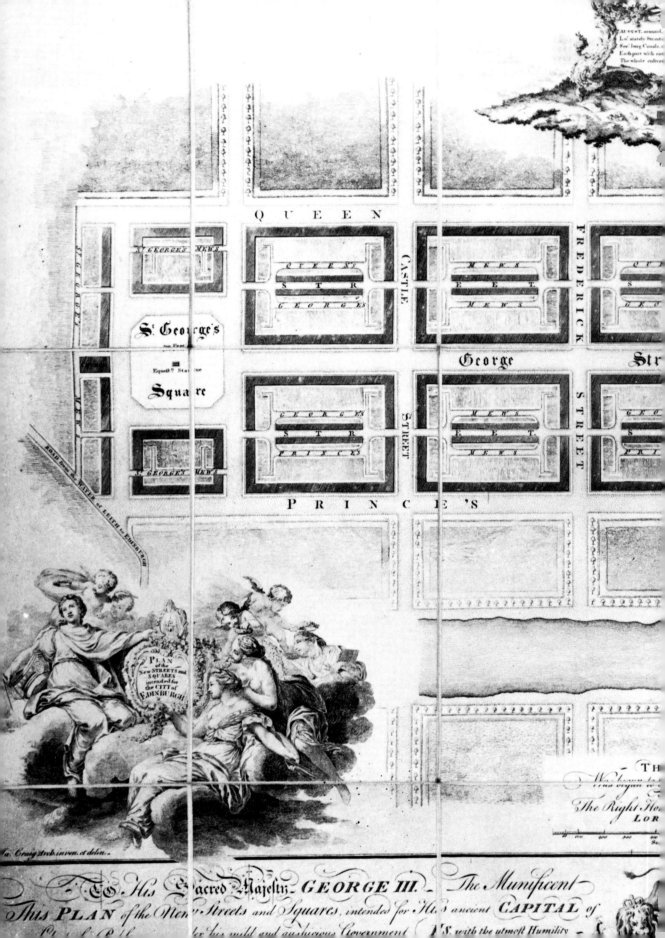

QUEEN

St GEORGE'S MEWS

St George's

Equest? Statue

Square

St GEORGE'S MEWS

CASTLE

QUEEN'S

STR

GEORGE'S

STREET

GEORGE'S

STR

PRINCE'S

FREDERICK

MEWS

STREET

STREET

MEWS

MEWS

GEORGE

Str

GEO

S

GEO

S

PRI

PRINCE'S

ROAD from the WATER of LEITH to EDINBURGH

PLAN
of the
New STREETS and
SQUARES
intended for
the CITY of
EDINBURGH

Ja: Craig Arch. inven. et delin.

TH

The Right Hon

LOR

TO His Sacred Majesty GEORGE III. The Munificent

This PLAN of the New Streets and Squares, intended for His ancient CAPITAL of

under his mild and auspicious Government IS. with the utmost Humility